This book is blank ... on purpose!

blank page

blank page

blank page

blank page

blank page

blank page

blank page

blank page

blank page

blank page

blank page

blank page

blank page

blank page

blank page

blank page

blank page

blank page

blank page

blank page

blank page

blank page

blank page

blank page

blank page

blank page

blank page

blank page

blank page

blank page

blank page

blank page

blank page

blank page

blank page

blank page

blank page

blank page

blank page

blank page

blank page

blank page

blank page

blank page

blank page

blank page

blank page

blank page

blank page

blank page

blank page

blank page

blank page

blank page

blank page

blank page

blank page

blank page

blank page

blank page

blank page

blank page

blank page

blank page

blank page

blank page

blank page

blank page

blank page

blank page

blank page

blank page

blank page

blank page

blank page

blank page

blank page

blank page

blank page

blank page

blank page

blank page

blank page

blank page

blank page

blank page

blank page

blank page

blank page

blank page

blank page

blank page

blank page

blank page

blank page

blank page

blank page

blank page

blank page

blank page

blank page

blank page

blank page

blank page

blank page

blank page

blank page

Made in United States
Orlando, FL
15 January 2022

13479904R00061